More or Less?

Rick Baker

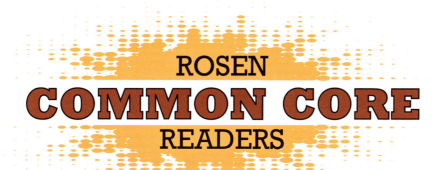

ROSEN COMMON CORE READERS

New York

Published in 2013 by The Rosen Publishing Group, Inc.
29 East 21st Street, New York, NY 10010

Copyright © 2013 by The Rosen Publishing Group, Inc.

All rights reserved. No part of this book may be reproduced in any form without permission in writing from the publisher, except by a reviewer.

Book Design: Michael Harmon

Photo Credits: Cover Artjazz/Shutterstock.com; pp. 5, 7 Inga Nielsen/Shutterstock.com; pp. 9, 11 Julian Rovagnati/Shutterstock.com; pp. 13, 15 (pizza box) Grauvision/Shutterstock.com; pp. 13, 15 (pizza slice) Ivan_Sobo/Shutterstock.com.

ISBN: 978-1-4488-8649-4
6-pack ISBN: 978-1-4488-8650-0

Manufactured in the United States of America

CPSIA Compliance Information: Batch #WS12RC: For further information contact Rosen Publishing, New York, New York at 1-800-237-9932.

Word Count: 24

Contents

More or Less? 4

Words to Know 16

Index 16

The jug has more.

The cup has less.

The boy has more.

The girl has less.

The box has more.

The plate has less.

Words to Know

box   cup   jug   plate

Index

box, 12
boy, 8
cup, 6

girl, 10
jug, 4
plate, 14